Business Leadership Blueprints

Jeffrey M. Bloom, EJD

Blane Friest

Todd Herschberg

Laura J. Lieff

Jane Tabachnick

www.SimplyGoodPress.com

A leader sees greatness in other people.
You can't be a leader if all you see is yourself.

Maya Angelou

Table of Contents

Introduction

There are natural born leaders, and there are those whose leadership abilities are within them - diamonds in the rough - waiting to be developed and fully realized.

The debate over whether great leaders are made or born has gone on for ages.

Stewart Friedman, in his newest book "Leading the Life You Want", explores the skills you need to be a leader. "One of the myths that I am trying to bust is that you are born with this capacity to be great. Not true. It is a matter of, yes, skill. There is a lot of luck. But there is also persistence, discipline, passion, and courage to pursue that which is most important to you and to the people around you."

Leaders are born, and leaders are developed. The five leaders profiled in this book come from a variety of backgrounds. They have taken different paths to become the leaders they are today. Using an interview format, the book helps discover their stories and their unique blueprints to becoming leaders.

Whether you are a business owner, a corporate manager, or an entrepreneur considering starting a business, you will benefit from reading the interviews with the five individuals profiled in this book. They each had a vision and followed it to fruition to become top leaders in business. These five professionals, Jeffrey M. Bloom, Blane Friest, Todd Herschberg, Laura J. Lieff, and Jane Tabachnick are the epitome of industriousness and innovation.

While some of the leaders simply fell into their specific line of work, the others were drawn to their field and devised powerful roadmaps that helped them to reach their end goal. In every case results were achieved, and these five subjects became recognized as leaders in their respective fields. As a totality, this group of five offers insight into entrepreneurship and self-sufficiency, resourcefulness and resiliency, as well as a calling to lead and to serve. Their stories form a blueprint for modern business seekers looking to find their own answers, and create their own paths to leadership.

Each chapter is like a lesson plan for action that is two-pronged. On the one hand, you hear how a person has taken their skills and talents forward to help others. On the other hand, you have a view of the clients who receive the benefits of interacting with the leader, from individuals, to corporate leaders to communities - both real and virtual.

Who are these entrepreneurs with spirit and ambition? The leaders you will meet are:

Jeffrey M. Bloom, who prides himself on fair and effective mediation services to a wide variety of clients. He helps people such as landlords and tenants, and divorcing couples, avoid the costly pitfalls of litigation, calming emotions and taming irrationality. He guides others in the art of taking control and achieving a positive outcome. He sees himself as a facilitator with the gift of bringing issues to a close with satisfaction.

Personal reward comes from breaking down barriers between people to build up sustainable results. No two cases are alike. Jeffrey brings his mediation skills to his leadership work - helping companies, individuals and organizations identify goals and plans, as well as build strong interpersonal relationships and skills to help them reach their target results.

For Blane Friest, it's The Maverick Way. He's done almost every job possible while working in the theater, as he felt this would best prepare him to be a better actor and director. Blane uses those finely honed skills to help entrepreneurs, executives and business owners express their unique brand and offerings on video. He knows how to use media to help people embrace their leadership selves and to find their own message and mission in the world. He knows that impacting family, friends, colleagues, and one's community is the answer to growth and advancement. Blane is curious and passionate about the world and uses storytelling, a universal language, to lead.

Todd Herschberg is the epitome of a person who has evolved over time in both his career and to become the leader he is today; from his early career writing code and algorithms to the savvy, passionate community building he does for both in person and virtual groups. Working primarily within the fashion and e-commerce realms, Todd's work runs deep into the heart of modern business. He cleverly helps lead Internet users into becoming top ambassadors of a brand. Creating such cheerleaders for an enterprise is a value proposition with great weight, as brands are now made and broken by their customers' online conversations. Todd also lends his time and leadership skills to a number of networking groups and charitable events.

Laura Lieff takes her insight into a different direction with coaching and concierge services. She aims to help those floundering lead more fulfilled and effective lives through her coaching. Her concierge service offers a perfect compliment, helping her busy clients who would otherwise struggle to juggle their days and nights without assistance. There is just too much stimulation and pressure for most to handle life alone. Laura makes it clear that she is not a psychologist, but a problem solver and guide to help people "let some fresh air into their brains."

Jane Tabachnick empowers her clients by ensuring they are seen as top experts in their niche, as well as creating media exposure that can put them on the map. Specializing in visibility and authority positioning, her approach is to lead clients from where they are, and support their individual goals and unique ways of doing business, to where they think they can go and beyond. She does this by offering mentoring, training, and education, as well as done for you solutions. "We like to say that we help our clients become the hunted, rather than the hunter; thus we turn them into client attraction magnets. This is what she refers to as "authority marketing"; for the businesses who are ready to take off, her programs provide rocket fuel-- giant boost and leverage-- that helps them get to the next level.

Five voices: five fonts of wisdom. Five people who want to help others achieve success. Each interviewee has found an individual answer to offer to the world. In this book, you will learn how it all started and where it is likely to go in the future. Each leader offers personal insight into their respective processes and proposed solutions. The art of the interview is used to document spontaneous stories and examples that can be seen as the hallmark of leadership. It is the ideal format to discover what makes leaders tick and how they have put in place their respective plans of action.

As much as the book deals with five different perspectives towards their clients, it also shows a commonality of leadership spirit. Finding one's inner go button that accounts for personal drive is the key. Something in the past sparks the present with inspiration. In seeing this in others, the reader will hopefully come to terms with what resides within his or her self.

Jeffrey M. Bloom, EJD

JEFFREY M. BLOOM, EJD

Tell me about My Mediation Services and the types of customers you help?

Jeffrey M. Bloom: I help people resolve conflicts, become better leaders and achieve positive results with a win-win strategy while helping them become the best possible versions of themselves.

In mediation, for example, a big part of my practice is family and divorce. I help couples through the process, to get resolved what has to be resolved so they can file for divorce or separation, or to handle pre- and post-divorce issues. In the end, they can have an agreement in place that works for both of them, not only now, but in the future. This is instead of going through the litigation process, hiring an attorney and spending $50,000 or more each, while losing control of the process along with their valuable time and money.

As a facilitator, I help them work through barriers and ensure that both parties have direct input and are in control of what goes into the final agreement. No one knows better than the couple what is best for themselves, their finances, or their children.

That being said, while they are not husband and wife anymore, they will always be Mom and Dad to their children. As a child of divorced parents, I know how important this is. Looking back, I hardly remember a time when my parents were not fighting or arguing about something. They finally divorced when I was 12 years old, and that did not make things any easier. It is true that divorce is always more emotional for the children, no matter how old they are. Couples should always have the best interests of their children at heart when deciding whether to separate or divorce.

It is so much easier for people to abide by an agreement when they have had input into and control over the process instead of having someone else, such as a judge or attorney, tell them what to do. With litigation, there is a greater chance of both parties running out of money, which can result in one or both of them being forced to sign a stipulation of settlement that doesn't work for either of them.

At the end of the litigation process, if you are able to get that far two or more years later, a judge will review your case for 20 to 30 minutes and then make a decision based solely on the law. A judge or attorney, or any other third party, has no real idea what is best for you. So, now the litigation process is over and you have spent a total of two to five years and about $80,000. At some point, one of the parties cannot abide by the final decision either because of financial hardship or for another reason. What's next?

The other partner is forced to hire an attorney, pay a substantial retainer fee, and go to court again, incurring additional legal fees. This is much less likely to happen when both parties are in control of the settlement. During the mediation process, both parties have direct input into the language and clauses.

Going forward, they both have to live their separate lives, and they both have separate finances. They have separate places to live while still maintaining a solid relationship and helping raise their children.

In addition, I help resolve contract disputes, landlord/tenant issues, roommate issues, business divorce issues, and business disagreements. I have also gone into organizations/businesses and facilitated discussions in regard to an ongoing conflict. I have provided conflict resolution workshops and put in place systems/policies/ideas and procedures to help resolve present and future conflicts.

To summarize, I am a certified independent leadership trainer, a coach, and a speaker with the John Maxwell team. I provide leadership trainings, coaching sessions, and mastermind groups tailored specifically to each organization based on its concerns, goals, and outcome assessment. This process helps leaders become stronger and increases their productivity and influence while taking them to the next level.

Effective leadership is the ability to influence—nothing more, nothing less. Just because someone has the title of manager or supervisor does not automatically make them an effective leader.

"It is the capacity to develop and improve their skills that distinguishes leaders from their followers." -Bennie and Nanus

An organization is only as strong as its people. Everyone in an organization is important and unique. An effective leader understands and recognizes the strengths of their people and uses those strengths effectively to get the job done.

"It's improper for one person to take credit when it takes so many people to build a successful organization." -Jim Sinegal

I have the ability to meet with decision makers and talk about their goals. I ask, "What is your organization's culture and what would you like it to be? What do you see happening next year, in five years, or ten years and beyond? What are some of the issues in the organization now?" Then I tailor a program of seminar(s) or ongoing training. I have the experience and ability to follow up with an accountability program to ensure that the goals and outcomes that were important, along with the new policies and procedures that were put into place, are being used effectively.

Can you describe the clients with whom My Mediation Services works?

Jeffrey M. Bloom: Couples going through a divorce, landlord/tenant cases, contract disputes, roommate disputes, vendor-vendee disputes, and any situation in which there are disputes or conflicts to be resolved. The mediation process involves a lot less time, a lot less money, and more win-win results as opposed to litigation.

Successful corporations know the value of leadership—in particular, transformational leadership, in which they put into place effective training programs that result in significant and positive change. Higher and more effective leadership happens through change and by learning, understanding, and implementing effective concepts to not only influence people, but to really understand the corporate culture. The number-one thing here is creating value for your people. Each and every person in a corporation or organization is unique and important. No one leader is 100-percent effective at everything, but they are able to recognize strengths and weaknesses in themselves and others to effectively leverage time and effort to get the desired results.

"Hire the best staff you can find, develop them as much as possible, and hand off everything you possibly can to them." -John C. Maxwell

Once corporations and organization understand the value of leadership and influence, success is not far behind. Having a "fresh set of eyes" or a neutral third party observe, evaluate, and teach is valuable. When I go into an organization, I have the ability to see things to which people who have been there for years have become numb. I learned this technique many years ago.

Back then, while I was in high school and prior to my enlisting in the United States Air Force in 1981, I worked as a shift leader and then a manager at McDonald's. It is so easy to get caught up in the day-to-day activities and operations behind the counter and to very quickly lose track of what the customer is seeing. Every so often during my shifts, I would come out from behind the counter, go outside into the parking lot, walk around, observe what was going on, walk into the front door, and experience what the customer was viewing, from the attentiveness of the staff to the cleanliness of the lobby area. This was a very effective tool in helping me retain an overall focus.

Another great technique I used was, on my off days, going into other McDonald's or fast food places, ordering something, sitting in the lobby for an hour or two, and watching the shift manager run his shift and people. One can learn a lot just by observing and seeing what works and what doesn't.

What led you to this field?

Jeffrey M. Bloom: I was a litigation paralegal running a litigation department for a plaintiff personal injury law firm. I worked for an attorney who did real estate for about five years, and there came a time when he took over his dad's practice in Brooklyn. He was concerned that the firm had only two sources of revenue, and there were times when both were slow. What where we going to do to get more money into the firm? I said to him, "Look, let's look at no-fault divorce. We don't have to appear in court. It's a matter of completing an intake, preparing the pleadings, collecting the fees, and it's done in a couple of months." He liked the idea.

While I was conducting research into mediation, I said, "We could grab both sides of the spectrum here." I looked into it, paid for my own training, and kept up to date with the ADR/mediation field on a regular basis. We would have couples come in; I would mediate conflicts, get them to an agreement, and then draft the final document. The attorney would represent one of the parties for the no-fault divorce paperwork, file it in a court—and that was it. This was another revenue stream that made sense for the firm.

Literally two years later, toward the end of 2013, he was going in a different direction. He didn't think he wanted to continue with family law and mediation. He said to me, "Jeff, I know you just completed law school. You are working on your master's degree in negotiation and dispute resolution and you probably don't want to go back to being just a paralegal. Maybe we should come up with an exit strategy."

I thought about it and realized that I had put a lot of work and training into mediation. I enjoyed helping people and I felt that I was making a difference. He was right; I did not want to go back to being a paralegal. Luckily enough, I was working with a business strategic planner, Edward F. Gibbons, Jr., Ph.D. of Rockford Kingsley, Ltd. (www.rockfordkinglsey.

JEFFREY M. BLOOM, EJD

org), in preparing to someday go out on my own. It just so happened that the opportunity came sooner rather than later. I had systems in place. I went out on my own full time in 2014 and have been on my own since.

How did you get started in mediation?

Jeffrey M. Bloom: I first started a practice in family and divorce mediation. As most readers know, the divorce rate is very high; it is over 50 percent, 55 percent at times, or higher. Most people don't know, however, that mediation exists as an option. They automatically think that they have to go to an attorney, and this is just not true.

I can't tell you how many times people have said to me over the years, "Where were you five years ago?"

One guy said to me, "If I had killed my wife, I would be out of jail by now." You hear it all. While conducting research for a paper, I met with a woman who shared with me how she had gone through the legal process with over five years in litigation, spending over $120,000. She and her spouse depleted their three children's college funds and had to sell real estate just to pay the attorneys. It got to a point where they had no money left, and she was forced to sign a stipulation of settlement that didn't work for her.

The result was that her husband got custody of her children, and this was just after he had gotten out of jail because he physically abused her. It's crazy what happens when you go through the litigation process. You never know what a judge is going to decide, and no attorney worth their salt can guarantee a particular outcome. Think of OJ Simpson or Casey Anthony, who did not report her 2-and-a-half-year-old daughter missing until 30 days had passed. Anything can happen in court. Anything.

Attorneys generally have no skin in the game or incentive to settle a case. They look at an individual's income and net worth statement and they are already figuring out what they can bill. The larger law firms hold attorneys accountable for a certain amount of billable hours each month, quarter, and year. If the attorneys do not reach these goals, they are working for another firm somewhere else or are out of work.

I attended a seminar a few years ago and was presented to a lawyer by a mediator who had over 40 years of experience. He had been talking to a prominent family law attorney who said, "I don't take any cases where the assets aren't at least $500,000, because I am going to get $125,000, the other attorney will get $125,000, and the couple is going to be left with the remainder."

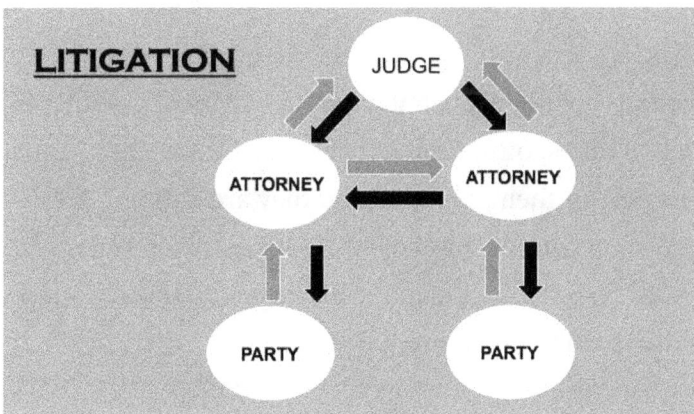

It is important to state here and now that not all attorneys operate like that; this example shows the far worse side of it, but this is not uncommon in litigation.

There are some attorneys who say something like this in response to a divorce request: "No problem, I'll get you that. You are entitled to this, you are entitled to that..." But they don't know what a judge is going to do. They don't know what is going to happen in depositions. They know what the law is, but they can't guarantee an outcome. People who are going through a divorce are emotional and they fall for these types of promises.

I have talked to couples in situations in which one wants to mediate and the other doesn't. "I don't want to go to mediation, and that's it. I am entitled to this and I am going to take you for everything you've got." Okay, what if that is true? What if the wife in this case is upset with the husband, and she gets him for everything because of something he did three years ago? After all the legal fees are paid at the end of the case, she can get only what is left. It doesn't make sense. Why cut off your nose to spite your face?

When emotions are high, it is not easy to be rational. Another huge myth involves when one spouse thinks that just because their husband/wife/partner cheated on them, for example, they are entitled to more money. This is simply not true and has no legal basis for determining the outcome of a case with respect to resolving child support, spousal support or the equitable distribution of the marital assets.

I very much enjoy mediation; no two cases are alike. The issues are similar, but the way parties react are very different. It's very rewarding when you get that occasional high-profile, high-conflict couple, where you think they'll never agree on anything. Then, working through the process for three or four sessions, or maybe a month or two later, they have a final agreement and one or both of them says, "Well, Jeff, you have helped us through a very emotional process. I can't believe you were able to help us work through this very difficult time and come to an agreement. Thank you very much."

The following depicts the mediation process. Both parties are in the same room as the mediator and there is a free exchange of ideas among all parties, making it so much easier to discuss and resolve issues.

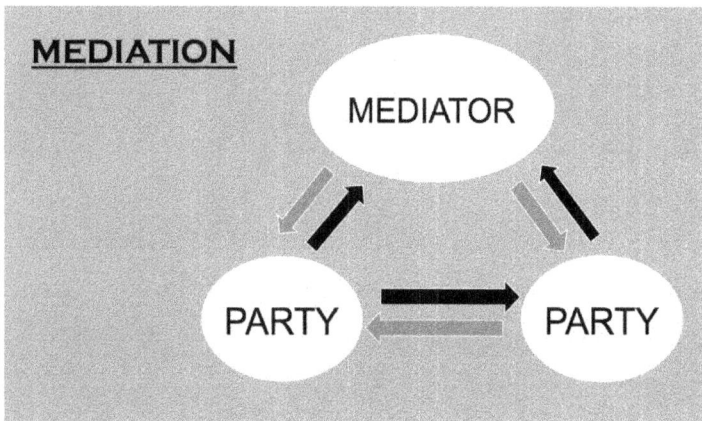

When I work with a couple, after all is said and done, they spend, on the average, less than about $6,000 on the total mediation process from start to finish. If they go through an attorney, the retainer fees are going to be from $15,000 to $25,000 each—and you know that this is not going to be all-inclusive.

In mediation, couples, businesses, groups, and organizations are in charge of the process. It is both rewarding and interesting, and I enjoy helping people and creating value in their lives. This is why I have added leadership training and seminars to my practice. I have also developed a non-profit organization called the Mediation Society of Long Island. As of the writing of this book, we are in the process of getting approval of our 501(C)3 status. It is going to be a mediation community center where we will provide mediation conflict resolution, conflict resolution skills, mediation, and leadership training, along with other educational and advocacy programs for those who cannot otherwise afford to pay for these valuable services.

Your commitment to using mediation as a leadership tool led you to additional training. Can you elaborate on this?

Jeffrey M. Bloom: Yes, as I mentioned, I am certified as an independent coach, teacher, and speaker with the John Maxwell team. I don't want to say that I fell into it, as I've always been interested in leadership. Over the years, I have listened to seminars and read books by Jack Canfield, Tony Robbins, John Maxwell, and Dr. Wayne Dwyer.

The reason I went with the certification program with John Maxwell is that he is someone who really cares about people. He leads by example and walks the walk; it is not just about words. When I was helping people resolve conflicts, going into small businesses and organizations, I thought about the next step. It was always at the back of my mind that there has to be accountability in terms of moving forward. People do not and cannot become better people and leaders just by reading books, attending a seminar(s), or going on a weekend retreat. Once all the hype and excitement dies down and you are back in your home or office, do you implement any of the strategies you learned, or do you go back to the way you were before and hope that everything changes via osmosis just because you attended the event or seminar?

How do you make employees better? This is why I took the next step and got my certification with the John Maxwell program. I attend training on a regular basis. I conduct mastermind groups, webinars, seminars, telephone conferences, or whatever a particular person, group, or organization requires.

What's the biggest misconception the reader may have about mediation or mediation and leadership?

Jeffrey M. Bloom: The biggest misconceptions and questions I hear about mediation are:

▶ When we both go to mediation, don't we both have to agree on anything/everything before we arrive?" That's not the case. For example, I have couples who come in with a list of 20 things that need to be resolved, and so far they have agreed on none. On the other hand, I have had couples come in with everything they have agreed upon; they just need to discuss how it's going to be drawn up. So this is a misconception.

▶ "Does the mediator have to be a lawyer?" Absolutely not. That's a big myth. Lawyers who are also mediators will tell prospective clients that a mediator must be an attorney. This is simply not true. If an attorney mediator is acting in the role of mediator, they can't give legal advice. They have to take off their lawyer hat and act as a neutral third party who has no vested interest in either side.

I advise prospective clients, "If you have questions, talk to an attorney or other mediators so you can make an educated decision." So you don't say five, ten, twenty years down the line, "Oh, I didn't know about mediation. I should have done it."

What is the most common obstacle preventing your clients from achieving great outcomes through mediation?

Jeffrey M. Bloom: To start, mediation is not a mandatory process; it is a voluntary process. I tell couples in the beginning that they are free to break off the mediation at any time. Everything we discuss in the mediation is strictly confidential. If the mediation breaks down and for whatever reason the parties both go to their own attorneys, my records can't be subpoenaed. I am not going to share anything discussed in the mediation process, nor can I be called as a witness for trial.

I have had two cases, maybe three, in my career, that have broken down such that one side did not want to continue with the mediation process. I remind them and say, "Look, you are free to leave, but what do you think is going to happen when you get an attorney?" When they start talking about it and realize what they are doing, more often than not, they sit back down and continue with the process.

You get some people who get whispered to in their ears by friends, acquaintances, and relatives: "My friend told me her husband makes the same amount of money you do and she has three kids, and she got this and she got that." The reality is, no two cases are alike. Assets, issues, and circumstances are different. There is no "cookie-cutter, one-size-fits-all" resolution when it comes to these issues.

I had someone call me a couple of weeks ago, as he and his wife had decided to divorce. I was trying to get them in for an appointment when he called and said, "Jeff, I am sorry but she said no way; she is not going through a mediator. She is going to take me for everything I got." This is exactly how he said it to me. He was the moneyed spouse. She didn't work for most of the marriage, so he would be on the hook for her legal fees as well as his own, in addition to spousal support—all of which can be more easily resolved through the mediation process.

If they both go to attorneys, he is going to be spending easily $50,000 to $100,000 each. So now the judge is going to say, "Okay, Jim, you are going to pay $1500 a month in child support and you have to pay $1800 a month in spousal support." Meanwhile, he has depleted all of his savings, retirement plan(s). You can't get blood from a stone, so what is he supposed to pay with? So he pays for a short period of time, maybe six months, a year, two years. At some point, he can't maintain this pace anymore. Then what does she do? She takes him back to court because he stopped making regular payments. She will have to retain another attorney or the same one, pay an initial retainer upfront, and then hope that she can recover the legal fees from her ex-husband. Her attorney will still get paid, and if her ex-husband does not have the financial ability to do so, then what? Litigation is an adversarial process in which the only parties who benefit are the attorneys.

Do you want the money to pay for your children's college fund, or for your attorney's children's college fund? There are some cases that are not fit for mediation, and litigation is the only choice. One very good example is if there is a case of domestic violence. If one party has an upper hand over the other, mediation will not be a fair, neutral process. The party without power will not be able to freely express their feelings and will just sit there and agree to everything to make the other party happy. People should be educated. They should know what their options are and see what works best for them.

Another myth just popped into my head. Sometimes someone will call and say, "My husband and I want to get divorced. We both agree that we want to get divorced and we want to go through mediation. Can I come and talk to you alone first?"

I don't allow this, and there is a very good reason why. As you are reading this situation, imagine that you call me and we talk about everything in regard to your case. Then you go back to your spouse and say, "Look, I just spoke to Jeff, a mediator. We have an appointment next week. We are going to get this resolved via the mediation process."

Almost immediately, the other spouse is going to say to himself or herself, "What did he/she tell Jeff? Jeff is now on his/her side." They won't come in: it just doesn't work. So I take as little information as possible on the phone and strongly suggest that they both be available for a three-way telephone conference or a free consultation in my office, where both of them can ask questions at the same time. This way, they can see that I am there to help both of them and not just one of them.

What is the biggest pitfall that the reader may not be aware of when it comes to leadership?

Jeffrey M. Bloom: The biggest pitfall in leadership is that you can read all the books you want, you can attend seminars, you can listen to tapes or CDs and watch DVDs, but unless you take action and start changing, then all that is for naught. You leave the weekend seminar all pumped up and excited, but if you don't have any takeaways from it and a plan of action, it is not effective. Everyone is where they are, whether great, good, or bad, because of the way they have done things up to this point in their lives. Results can change only when action changes. Do you plan out your day? What are your priorities? What are your outcomes? What are you looking for when you are planning things? What are your desires? It just doesn't happen by itself and it doesn't happen by not taking action.

"Having a powerful enough WHY will provide you with the necessary HOW." -Tony Robbins

People will use this as an excuse: "I want this, I want that, but I don't know how to do it. So forget it." People tell them they can't do something, and for some reason they believe it and give up. If you literally have a powerful enough why, whatever the goal is—whether you want to own your own business or you want to be a better father, a better mother, get a better job—in finding the necessary how, you will figure out a way to do it. People have done things in their lives where they justified something and although it seemed impossible, somehow they were able to produce the desired result. They figured out the why and the how.

When you have things to do, until they become a MUST, they will not get done. We have all heard it before. I SHOULD lose weight, I SHOULD stop smoking, I SHOULD get a better job. You wind up "shoulding" all over yourself. Positive results happen when something becomes a must for you and when you are sick and tired of being sick and tired.

How can the reader avoid or overcome these obstacles to successfully achieve business leadership through mediation?

Jeffrey M. Bloom: Business leadership and mediation are two different things, but similar principles are used with the goal of teaching people how to listen and talk to become better versions of themselves. With business leadership, I go into organizations and provide trainings and seminars to facilitate change. Mediation is where I help resolve conflict and help parties come to a solution.

In regards to mediation, no two cases are alike. While the issues are the same, couples handle them differently. You can have issues that you would think are the toughest things in the world to facilitate, and it is easy for one couple, and not so easy with another. I had a couple argue literally for an hour about who was going to get a $40 vacuum cleaner. I knew in my experience as a mediator that it really wasn't about the vacuum cleaner. So, I had to get in there and get to the underlying issue, to see what was really going on. I couldn't just say, "Here's $40; buy another vacuum cleaner." That is not the role of the mediator.

What would be the best advice to the reader who is considering mediation?

Jeffrey M. Bloom: The best advice I have is, when considering mediation, learn as much as you possibly can about it. If you don't know what mediation is, just do some research so you can make an educated decision. I offer a free consultation in which couples come to my office to see if we are a fit for each other. You need to do your homework. If you think an attorney is the best way to go, talk to a couple of them and weigh your options. See what works best for you in your situation. Don't let somebody tell you, "Oh, you should go to mediation or you should go to litigation." Only you can make that decision.

What is the first thing a reader should do if they are ready to start mediation?

Jeffrey M. Bloom: If they decide to go through the mediation process, they need to start getting everything in order. A good mediator will give you a checklist of all the documents they need in order to ensure complete disclosure.

Be willing to sit in a room together. At some point you loved each other enough to get married, and you spent many years together, and you have children. Therefore, there is no reason why you can't sit in a room together for a couple of hours at a time before moving on. It doesn't mean that you have to agree with the other person. However, when you are in a room together and you are able to exchange ideas with the mediator, it's much different than discussing something among yourselves, which more often than not results in an argument. Sometimes, when I get the initial phone call, it is one spouse. One of the questions I ask is, "Is your wife or husband on the same page?"

The response might be: "She/he doesn't really know." "I haven't really told him/her yet." Or, "They have an idea, so how do I bring this up?"

I always tell them, "You have to bring up the discussion, but don't do it at home because it is not a neutral environment. Go out to dinner. Maybe go shopping." Be in a neutral place where there is usually less chance of an argument or conflict.

What is the most important thing the reader should think about if they are about to go into mediation in a business negotiation, a meeting, or team building?

Jeffrey M. Bloom: Members of an organization may be going into a team building session or a meeting in which they want to be productive. You have to be prepared. You can't go in without an agenda, or without goals or outcomes. How many of us have been to a business meeting where literally nothing gets accomplished? Or maybe there is an agenda and two of the items get checked off, and the only result is that nothing important was accomplished and you have wasted the organization's resources by having 10 or more employees away from their work for two hours, for a total of 20 hours of productivity. Why have a meeting just to have a meeting? You must plan for what people can expect to take away and implement.

In business relations, in meetings, or in going into a negotiation, whatever the case may be, you have to have an idea of what your desired outcome is. There are terms called BATNA and WATNA. BATNA is your "best alternative to a negotiated agreement" and WATNA is your "worst alternative to a negotiated agreement." Everyone who goes into a mediation or negotiation may know what their best possible scenario is and what their worst possible scenario is. Sometimes the result is something in between, but by understanding this, you can be better prepared.

How can a reader find out more about how to use mediation or conflict resolution skills as a leadership tool, or as part of a leadership tool?

Jeffrey M. Bloom: In the realm of organizations, a mediator or a conflict resolution specialist can be retained; this person comes in as a neutral third party with the requisite experience and fresh eyes to facilitate an ongoing conflict or to teach conflict resolutions skills, and, if need be, to help with follow-up skills to make sure that processes are working.

A company's first response might be, "Well, we have a human resources department for that." Yes, you have human resources, but it isn't a neutral third party; they have a vested interest in corporate goals and outcomes. The only way to effectively resolve a conflict is to hire somebody from the outside. A true neutral third party can observe, facilitate, and talk to people on all sides.

I use the term "business ombudsman." Most people know this from nursing homes and hospitals. The ombudsman is a neutral third party who doesn't answer to anyone other than the two sides. They talk to patients about their concerns and then report to management or to the employees on a strictly anonymous basis. We solve issues in a similar way, so that somebody is not afraid to say something or to make a complaint out of fear that they are going to get fired or that there is going to be retribution.

What is the best way for the reader to learn more about your work?

Jeffrey M. Bloom: They can visit my website, where I have an FAQ page with a lot of information, at mymediationservices.com. There are other websites that talk about mediation and mediators. If you decide to go to mediation or litigation, or to leadership training, I advise that you meet with the key person one on one and see what they have to offer—if there is a fit for you and your organization. The only way the process is going to be effective is if you feel comfortable with that person, whether it be me or someone else.

If the reader thinks they might be ready, how can they connect with you?

Jeffrey M. Bloom: They can call me. My office number is (516) 308-7808. They can email me at jbloom@mymediationservices.com. I always return calls immediately unless I am in a session. Then I will return calls within a couple of hours or before the end of the day. I am always available to talk on the phone, answer questions, or have people come in for a free in-office consultation. I would like to add that the parties do not have to be in the New York area, as I offer online dispute resolution (ODR).

Anything else you want to add?

Jeffrey M. Bloom: Everybody should be educated before making an important decision in regards to a divorce, separation, child custody issue, support issue, contract dispute, or any type of dispute that needs the help of a mediator to get a workable resolution. The automatic steps should not be, "I have to get an attorney and spend a lot of money and a lot of time." Alternative dispute resolution (ADR) is a way that people can resolve their conflicts and issues without going through all that aggravation and cost with a possible lose-lose or win-lose situation.

BIO – Jeffrey M. Bloom, EJD

Jeffrey M. Bloom is a mediator/facilitator and conflict resolution specialist and leadership coach, speaker and trainer. His mission is to add value in helping people resolve conflict, become better leaders and achieve positive results with a WIN/WIN strategy, while becoming the best possible version of themselves.

- Served honorably in the United States Air Force for over 16 years

  Deployed for both Desert Storm and Iraqi Freedom

- John Maxwell Independent Certified Coach, Speaker, Trainer

- New York Center for Mediation and Training

- Executive Juris Doctorate from Concord Law School

- Master's Degree in Negotiation and Dispute Resolution from

  Creighton Law School

- Facilitator with SOLIYA

SOLIYA facilitates an online cross-cultural education program with students from over 100 universities in 27 countries across the Middle East, North Africa, South Asia, Europe and North America. This program empowers the emerging community of young adults to amplify voices from civil society that are not commonly heard and catalyze constructive and respectful discourse across divisions about important socio-political issues.

JEFFREY M. BLOOM, EJD

Contact information:

Phone: (516) 308-7808

Email: jbloom@mymediationservices.com

Website: www.mymediationservices.com

Blane Friest

Tell me about The Maverick Way and the types of customers you help.

Blane Friest: The Maverick Way has been a multi-year search. It has been about trying to figure out my space and what kind of leader I am and where my passions lie. It's about how I take my passions and the things that really get my juices flowing and put it all into the world.

The Maverick Way came out of a Sally Hogshead process called The Fascinate Test. It came out that I was the maverick leader. I remember feeling this incredible sense of relief. At that moment, I felt permission to really go out and be who I was. I come from a very stoic culture (I'm Scandinavian American). Showing emotions is not welcome in my community. It can be very dangerous. I've always felt like I never really fit in.

This whole concept of the maverick is someone who goes out into the world. I always see a maverick as a traveler. My favorite thing is to travel. I love traveling the world and meeting people. I love immersing myself in other cultures and seeing what I can learn from them. To me, this is part of the maverick way--taking myself outside of the normal way of being, and turning it into something.

The kind of people I like to work with are creatives. When I say that, I don't want to put them into a box. To me, a creative leader is anyone who creates anything. It's not only an artist and it doesn't have to be an actor or a director or a painter. Anyone who has an idea and has the guts to go out on a limb and try something and really commit to it, are the kind of people I like to work with.

The Maverick Way for me is stepping out of what was probably prescribed for me in my life, which would have been a very safe living, into something somewhat dangerous. I travel a lot. I scuba dive. I jump out of airplanes. That's the kind of activity that gets my passion going, along with starting a new business. These are the people that I really like to help. I love getting their ideas aligned and getting them started. I just did a three-day intensive with a client /friend and we completely re-branded her business and gave her a six-month to-do list. I'll be checking up with her every week. She now has all this great, renewed energy in what she is doing.

A terrifying space to be as a leader, a business owner, or an entrepreneur is to get to that place where you say, "Okay, I've been growing comfortably and I have kind of plateaued, so what do I need to do to actually instill new energy into my business?" The bottom line is that most businesses fail within the first three years. If you are making a living after this point, you are one of less than ten percent of the survivors in the startup community. That's a really dangerous place to be because the second you get complacent in that three to five year space is when you start to die as a business. I love working with these people and really challenging them.

I work a lot with people's fears. I ask, "What are you afraid of?" I'm going through this with my production company right now, which is on the cusp of a new space. I'm struggling myself with the fear of, "Okay, I'm going to need three to five new employees in the next year." That terrifies me. I'm taking responsibility for other people's lives.

Describe the client The Maverick Way works with.

Blane Friest: I work with people who are starting up. One of the things that I've fallen into in the past, is there are people who start up with passion and no money. This is an interesting group of people to help. I love helping people figure out how they can finance their ideas. I actually have a lot of connections with people in the fundraising world--the crowd sourcing space, and they are really exciting. I like to work with people who have a great idea, or people who are in a business that needs to transition, or achieve a space of growth.

What led you to this field?

Blane Friest: That's a huge question. I started out acting and directing, which is the area I got my degree in. I immediately graduated college and started to work as a lighting designer. I always knew that I wanted to be a producer of some sort. Initially, I started touring with theater groups, and a little bit of music. I wanted to explore the world. I also knew that if I wanted to be an effective producer, I also needed to do every job in the business. I'm not great with hair and makeup, but otherwise I've done most everything. Once I got to that point, I started my production company.

As the production company started to expand, I realized that I felt a little hemmed in. About ten years ago, I started meditating and practicing Buddhism. I started to open up to the fact that I really want to help people find who they are, find their own voice, and help them express it. Ironically, it goes all the way back to when I started as an actor and director. How do you stand on stage in front of hundreds if not thousands of people and connect with every individual there? How do I form my message so that people actually get interested in me?

My belief is consistent with Sally Hogshead's that if I am more connected to my passion, my message and what I really feel is my purpose in life, then the right people are going to be attracted to me. For me, that's leadership. Being consistent and being confident in that consistency, that's a piece of leadership.

I still have my production company, which I love. As I've said, it's growing, but I've really become fascinated with the creative pursuits of starting up a business. If I'm aligned with your business or you are able to tell me your story in a way that interest me, then I am definitely more interested in working with you.

How did you get started in the business?

Blane Friest: I started taking a lot of coursework in leadership. I learned some concepts from Jack Canfield. My Zen teacher has created something called the Big Mind Western Zen process, which combines traditional Zen and Buddhist teachings with western psychotherapeutic practices. I found it to be genius. I found a mentor who is an extremely successful leadership development person and an individual coach. He has a very few individual clients, but otherwise, he speaks to large groups of people on leadership. He is extraordinary. I started to get some coaching from him and then started coaching friends.

A friend of mine came to me completely unsolicited and said, "Hey, I've watched you start your own couple of successful businesses and I want you to help me do it." This was about five years ago. She is extremely successful right now. As I started to open up to this, people started to come and ask me to mentor them. It really started out with mentoring some people and then realizing that I actually had some aptitude for it. These people's lives were changing.

I was thinking about something this morning. I grew up in a small town in Iowa. My mother was a home economics teacher and back then, seven hundred years ago, the home ec teacher in a small town was really the one who did most of the student counseling. If you wanted counseling, you would go to the school guidance counselor for help with your class work or if you needed guidance on how to put together a resume. If a student needed advice dealing emotions or living, you would send them to the home ec teacher. My mother started to get a little overwhelmed with this, so she and I created what we called a peer counseling program.

We developed a program, which last I've heard is still being used in my high school, twenty-seven years later. That's when I actually started mentoring people. I just realized how much I loved mentoring, teaching and helping people. It was very much about finding out what people's fears are, what's getting them stuck, and then helping them work through it. I was doing this even when I was in eighth grade with younger kids in our school system.

How did you get started in branded television?

Blane Friest: When I started out, I had this idea of a production company and then a coaching business, but there was a gap between them. Over the course of about the first year or so, it became really clear that by separating these two passions of mine, neither one was really benefiting. I asked myself, "How do I put these things together?" Here I am practicing Zen and trying to help people find their true authentic selves and mode of self-expression.

It really was taking my twenty plus years of professional experience in production and putting it together with my leadership development and my coaching. Initially, one of the first products I created was something I called Video Manifesto. I use the structure of a Shakespearean five-act play--bam, bam, bam, bam, bam. It's really clear. It nails who am I, what I do, and who is my client. A person speaks directly to the client and tells him or her why am I the best person to serve in this particular area. This became a really powerful tool for my clients and I began to interview.

I created my first television show, an online YouTube show called Talks With Transformers. Some of the interviews were my clients, some of them were not. Then I found that I was able to take a lot of these pieces from the interviews and actually edit them down into teaching moments, where I help build an entire social media campaign around this content. The statistics keep growing about shows how powerful video is in marketing.

Asking questions while interviewing people and helping clients pull ideas out has become a very effective marketing tool, a branding tool to get them established as an expert and gets their methods out into the world. My largest production company clients are in finance and pharmaceuticals. I love the world of finance--how Wall Street works and the International Monetary Fund. I'm also a maverick. What I love to do is find people who might be working and tweaking ideas and systems in that industry. I spent some time in that industry as well, and was even licensed for a short period of time before I moved to New York.

I love to find people who have unique methods that might be a bit disruptive of the status quo and the old ways of doing things. I have to be a little careful because I do have very large financial institutions who are clients. In a lot of ways, Wall Street works in terms of our whole culture is not in fact working. It's working for a very, very small group of people while the rest of us are struggling more and more every day just to maintain a middle class existence. To me, how does an individual or a very small company compete with a multi-trillion dollar organization? They are not going for the same clients, but how do you get heard? The whole idea of branded television is "who I am." Utilizing what can be very inexpensive and often times free to communicate a message is powerful, including social media and YouTube. How do you find speaking engagements? How do you get out there and tell your story?

How did The Maverick Way show come about?

Blane Friest: That's an interesting story. I mentioned previously about developing Talks With Transformers. I rented a space in the city for my business. I had four types of entrepreneurs come in. That show never really took off, but it was a giant learning experience for me. We did actually create some really good, effective and useful things for most of the people. All of them are using what we did.

One of the great ironies in life is that you can really coach someone, mentor someone, but you completely forget to apply it to yourself. During a three-day intensive with a client, I mentioned the Fascinate Test and how The Maverick Leader was my thing. A light bulb went off in my head. We actually ended up putting her work on hold and worked together on my concept because she is a coach.

That's how The Maverick Way show came about. We realized that there was something missing. I had lost my passion for work. My two greatest passions in life are travel and adventure, and meeting people. My other real true passion in life is food. I love cooking.

I have become very good friends with Michael Pollan, nominated for Secretary of Agriculture. The media attention has allowed him to tell his story, "Okay, this is what the food industry is in the country." In any case, my passion for food and for meeting people, and my passion for travel all started to come together. I remember as a kid, I used to love a show that would come on television on Sunday mornings -- On the Road with Charles Kuralt. I thought that I needed to take this idea and turn it into a mass shift. The idea of The Maverick Way is to find people who are doing things, even some disruptive things, or trying something new--people who are swimming against the stream, people who are really going for it and are getting some energy going. The Maverick Way show is meant to go to them.

One of the things I want to shoot is share a meal with people. It doesn't necessarily need to be an entire meal. We sit down and we have a cup of coffee and they tell me their story and all about their creative process.

Food is a great way to connect with the community especially utilizing all the new media; it really is stepping away from marketing. I find out what their life is about. That's what The Maverick Way show is.

What is the biggest misconception the reader may have about branding and leadership?

Blane Friest: I think that branding and leadership are two completely different things. A leader leads people and runs something, but branding is the label you put on a business. Branding is not quite as bad as the term "marketing." The term branding can be manipulative. Because of this, there's a little bit of denying the importance of creating a personal brand going on. It doesn't need to be. What I do when I'm working with a leader is to ask, "What is your personal mission statement? What is your personal vision statement? What is your passion?"

I've worked with a woman by the name of Janet Attwood, who created something called The Passion Test. I'm a certified passion test facilitator. It's another tool I've gathered over time. People start to get a lot of clarity about their passions and mission in the world. Then as a leader I ask how does this fit into your leadership? I believe very strongly that leadership is building community. It's being clear about your own message and who you are in the world, to your family, to your employees, and to your community. The right people who are connected and aligned with you in your personal brand are going to be attracted to you; it might be partners, it might be employees, and it will be customers.

The biggest misconception is that it involves two different perspectives: one is client or world facing. The other is something inside you or the business and how you deal with employees. You are going to be running a business, whether you are a solo entrepreneur, a small business, or a leader of a giant business; and there's going to be a disconnect when you separate the two views.

There's an awful lot of communication that happens among people. Studies say that eighty-five plus percent is non-verbal and has nothing to do with words. If your words are inconsistent with the rest of your communication about who you are, then there's going to be a disconnect. I believe very strongly that you are not going to grow the way you should. You are not going to actually impact your community, your family, and your employees effectively.

One of the greatest leaders I've ever seen is the guy who started the company BlackRock. His name is Larry Fink and he is one of the greatest leaders I have ever seen. I watched him speak to about three hundred and fifty of his right-out-of-school new hires. Somebody asked him a question and he told a story that really bared himself to these people. This guy runs a multi-trillion dollar business and he is standing there being a human being and I feel that this transcends the entire organizational unit. It's an organization of twelve, thirteen thousand employees with lots and lots of assets under management and offices literally blanketing the globe.

When I see him, there's actually a human being there. He is being true to himself and his passion. He is always talking about integrity and the financial system. I think he is doing a lot of amazing work to help fix some of the issues I've identified in the past as things not working in the world.

What's the most common obstacle preventing the reader from achieving great outcomes through branding and leadership?

Blane Friest: Fear is a human being's greatest obstacle. Most people are more driven by fear than anything else. It's not like we've run through the world terrified of everything, but it's that we all have our own issues. They are all unique to us. One of the things I do as part of my Buddhist/Zen practice is to explore how to find balance, how to hold to supposedly opposite ideas. You might be a great leader, but then what fear is keeping you from going to the next level? What beliefs about yourself are not allowing you to really get your message out into the world and grow as fast as you potentially can in order to impact your community in the best way possible?

It often revolves around the fear of being embarrassed and the fear of failure. My biggest fear in the world is of being laughed at, being embarrassed in public. So I put myself on TV and get up and talk to as many people as I possibly can. As I've said before, I've jumped out of airplanes and I go scuba diving and do all sorts of crazy stuff. That's because I really like to play with that whole fear thing. Everybody's fears are unique except that we all have them in common. Those fears are controlling us in particular areas of our lives. We are holistic creatures. If my relationship with my partner isn't working, it's really, really difficult to shut that part of my life off and come into work and be an effective leader there.

If I'm having a hard time communicating with my partner because of something I'm afraid of, I'm going to have the same issues communicating with my management team and the leaders within my organization. When I work one-on-one with an individual, I ask: What is holding you back?

What are your fears and how are they affecting you? I guarantee you that those same fears are affecting your relationships with your family. It impacts you and how you are seen in your community. It carries over into your work.

What's the biggest pitfall the reader may not be aware of?

Blane Friest: We know what we know. We know what we don't know, but then we don't know what we don't know. I think the pitfall here is where you get into a state of mind where you think you know something and you think you are right about something. That is the most dangerous place to be. The second you think you have figured something out, you are in trouble. I think this tends to leads to complacency. It's like the entrepreneur who has figured out his or her business. You are making money and you are comfortable and happy.

Ironically, Larry Fink said this to his group, "There are an awful lot of people who have been with the business, ten, twelve years and they are making more money than they ever thought they would. They are happy and their families are great. They've got great homes and they really, really love their jobs. I want to fire those people."

He is not saying he is going to out and firing all the happy people in his business, but his point is that the second you think you have it figured out, you are in trouble. I just want people to understand that when you start to feel complacent, negative things are going to start happening. Your mind might be a little dull and you might not be quite as clear. It's not like life or owning a business has to be torture, but you definitely need to stay on your toes.

How can the reader avoid or overcome this obstacle to successfully achieve business leadership through branding?

Blane Friest: Both my parents were high school teachers. My dad was a basketball coach. I think that everyone, especially every leader, needs someone that they can really talk to and hopefully that person will challenge them. I almost hate the word coach now because it's been so overused and everybody on earth is a coach these days. Everyone needs someone in their lives who can speak to them honestly that can really be straight with them.

When you get complacent, you need someone to point out that you are being this way, and then maybe they will inspire you to identify where that complacency is taking you--maybe move you to push your boundaries a little bit. It could be your pastor or your priest. I know that there are so many people who have a really solid spiritual foundation. Buddhism and Zen seem to make sense to me. You really need someone in your life, be it someone you hire or a family member. I know so many people whose spouses or romantic partners fill this role for them.

What would be the best piece of advice to the reader who is considering branding and leadership?

Blane Friest: Find someone to follow, go online and research, or read a book that will help. The simple answer is to connect to your passion. Why are you here? Why are you doing what you are doing? If you find that you are doing something inconsistent with your passion in life, then take a good look at it. Go through the process of creating a personal vision and mission statement. The Passion Test is an extremely simple and valuable tool. There are number of these tools online. Make yourself open. Put yourself out there. Tweak yourself. Do something that might scare the hell out of you. But make sure that you are having fun in life.

If you are not enjoying things, you are not going to approach them with passion. There is another thing that has been identified to me that I tend to lack. I've had more than one of my coaches tell me is be clear about my why. A lot of people have children. A lot of people have a family. I donate money to Kiva, which is an organization that gives tiny little micro loans to people all over the world. Find something that is your why, that inspires you, that's going to keep you moving forward.

What's the first thing the reader should do if they are ready to start branding or evolving their branding?

Blane Friest: The first thing they should do is sit down and figure out their why. I think the Passion Test is a great way to do this, or you can go online and find other resources. If you are not clear as to what a vision and a mission statement are, read up on it. They are really very simple.

The mission statement is more action-based and the vision statement is where you want to be at some point. In writing your personal vision and mission statements, you should see the big picture. You might find it really difficult, but just the process is going to start you on the path of really finding out who you are--your true expression of your true self and where your space is in the world. What may well come up are things that are missing in your life.

What's the most important thing the reader should think about if they are about to go into branding themselves?

Blane Friest: The correct answer for the last one might be: don't try to do it yourself. You can do some of this work, but at some point you really need outside help. I think a lot of people try to create their own personal brand and deal with it. If you are spending time and energy and you are really good at it, creating your personal brand and that for your business is great. Maybe you should do this for a living. It's really important that you understand that you need to run your business, whatever that business is. Somewhere, there are people who are really good at this and far more efficient than you might be. Go get some help. Don't worry about delegating this piece.

How can the reader find out more about how to use branding as a leadership tool?

Blane Friest: That's an awesome question. We are talking about branding-the colors of your brand and your logo, including the right fonts. That's how you present yourself to the world. Turn it on its head and think of branding from the point of view of a community building tool. Once you do this, you'll bring a lot of fresh ideas into what your brand might be as an individual or as a business.

The larger businesses literally pay tens, if not hundreds of millions of dollars a year to make sure that the way they present themselves to the world is clear and consistent with who they are and what they want to be. To really internalize it, think, "How do I use this branding to attract the right kind of partners, the right kind of employees, the right kind of customers?" Branding is really the first step. It's like an introduction to you and your business. From a customer point of view, your goal is to turn your customers into raving ambassadors for your business. First of all, that's not everybody. There are people for whom you can do really, really great work who are not going to turn into ambassadors for you and these may not be the kind of clients you want.

You want the kind of clients who are going to be excited to work with you and will then turn around and tell everybody how great you are. Branding is like an introduction to the great client, the right employee, and the community around you. What is my impact on my community? Maybe it's my neighborhood or my town or my city or my country, or even the whole world. You have to ask how do you approach them from a community standpoint.

What's the best way for the reader to learn more about your work?

Blane Friest: You can go online and you can go to the YouTube channel, Talks With Transformers. I'm always open for an e-mail at blane@ ddmproduction.com. We can find some time to talk if you are really interested in doing some work. Over the time of my training, what I've discovered about myself is that I can be pretty laser focused. Everything may not be a game and be pleasant. But if we work together, we are going to have fun because that's how I like to do business. There might also be times when I will go at those pieces of you and your business and it might not be the most comfortable experience in the world. You have to be willing to push yourself outside of your comfort zone if you want to work with me, because that's where the magic happens.

If the reader thinks they might be ready, how they can connect with you?

Blane Friest: Shoot me an e-mail. They can always call my business and leave a message at 212-575-2482. If someone really thinks they have unique qualities and things that might make for an interesting episode of The Maverick Way, please call. We are always looking for interesting people doing interesting things in interesting places.

BIO – Blane Friest

Blane, a serial entrepreneur having started his first business at 13, is an avid traveler and explorer, and to make a living, is an actor/director/ producer and talk show host, an inspirational speaker and Executive Coach specializing in entrepreneurship, small business transformation and community building.

As founder of DDM Production LLC, Blane loves leading teams in producing unique and cutting edge C-suite events for many Wall Street firms. Blane's favorite position was as Adjunct Professor for the Carroll College (now Carroll University) Theatre Dept and Production Manager for the school's International Tour of Ionesco's Rhinoceros performed in Moscow and Tashkent, Uzbekistan. He is also a teacher of Zen and facilitator of the Big Mind Western Zen Process™ and a Certified Facilitator of the Passion Test.

As an Iowa native, Blane is a lifelong food enthusiast and passionate food activist since reading Michael Pollan's book, Omnivore's Dilemma. Shortly after the President Obama's election, Blane was inspired to write the 'Pollan for Secretary of Agriculture' petition that garnered both national and international media attention. Blane continues to use his unique perspective as a man who grew up in a small rural community working on farms who now works on (or more accurately, around) Wall St. --- to spread the principles of the importance of supporting local economies through building communities.

Blane's new project, The Maverick Way, is the all-encompassing expression of his life's passions - food, travel and making messes. In the TV series, Blane travels the US (soon, the world) shares meals with and tells the stories of 'Maverick disrupters' and their communities. The show is scheduled to be followed by a book and International Tour in which Blane will share how these brave entrepreneurs are committed to changing the world (usually for good), the lessons learned, and grow the worldwide 'Maverick' community. His greatest challenge in creating 'The Maverick Movement' is saying the show's name without hearing the voice of a certain ex- Governor of Alaska and Presidential candidate in his head. The other voices have yet figured out how to drown that one out.

Contact Information:

Phone: 212-575-2482

Email: blane@ddmproduction.com

Website: www.thesizzle.com

Todd Herschberg

Tell me about Quantimark and the types of customers you help?

Todd Herschberg: Over the years, Quantimark has helped a large number of customers, but our primary focus is helping companies, specifically those with enterprise scale data. Retailers build communities they can engage with, market to and use the user-generated community content to help them rank better in search engine listings.

Describe the client that Quantimark works with?

Todd Herschberg: Quantimark mostly works with two types of clients. The first one is in the fashion industry, primarily in women's apparel, but generally any sort of fashion will work. The second type is the e-commerce company. Clearly there is a lot of overlap, but generally with e-commerce, we're dealing with enterprise scale, so there are millions of products.

What led you to this field?

Todd Herschberg: I stumbled into the field, starting out in the prehistoric days writing algorithms for early search engines. I was the math guy, and my job was to write algorithms to help companies with page ranking. I then moved over to the marketing side, taking what I knew about how search engines worked and opened up my own SEO consulting practice, which eventually became Quantimark.

As the algorithms grew and were refined with Google, Yahoo, Bing, Baidu in China, and all of the larger engines, it became clear that to rank well, you needed a large amount of content. To create, there are two routes you can go. Number one, you can sit down and hire a team of a million writers to create millions of pages of content. The other route is to engage and build a community that will generate that content for you, free of charge.

How did you get started in the business?

Todd Herschberg: I got started in the business by accident. I had been an engineer, writing code for one of the early search engines, writing the algorithms that helped pages rank internally; and from there, I moved over to the other side, taking what I knew to help clients rank better.

How did you get started in SEO and community building?

Todd Herschberg: I had been doing traditional SEO, and one of the key pieces of search engine optimization is to have content that will rank well on specific terms. You hire writers to do what you tell them, or you can build a community to write what they call user-generated content. It's infinitely scalable and it tends to include terms that you would never think of giving your writers, since your community is writing about what they care about rather than what you're researching.

How did the community building service come about?

Todd Herschberg: The community building service came about originally by accident. A large amount of my career has been by accident, but I had started by creating a small group when I was working as the marketing director for a men's apparel company. We were selling men's neckwear, which is a niche space as fewer and fewer people wear ties. I felt it would be good to try to build a community on LinkedIn called the

Well Dressed Professionals, figuring this would allow me to find a group of self-identified as people who were likely to wear ties. I said to myself, "Oh, I'll grab these people, I'll identify them; I'll market to them."

It turned out that the content they were creating actually generated significant traffic, not just for those users within the group, but in bringing in other people who were not initially members. People were stumbling across those pages looking for neckwear or for tie pins, tie clips, etc., and that's when the light bulb went off. "Ah. This may be a really good thing to scale across my clients."

What's the biggest misconception the reader may have about community building?

Todd Herschberg: One of the biggest mis- conceptions is that it's very easy to build a community. Depending on the type of community, the level of engagement, and the goals, it can range anywhere from very, very simple to more complex. If all you need is a community of two people, it's very easy to do that. If you're trying to scale to a million people, it's a little harder. Leading people down the initial path to building a community and increasing engagement can be tricky.

This is where Quantimark comes in. We help navigate those initial stumbling blocks. Once you've got a community that reaches a certain threshold (and that threshold will vary from industry to industry and group to group), you'll find that what they call the network effect kicks in and that group will be pretty well self-policing and self-sustaining. The amount of effort you'll require is minimized.

What is the most common obstacle preventing the reader from achieving greater outcomes from their community building?

Todd Herschberg: I think the greatest obstacle the typical client faces is trying to do this themselves. They say, "Hey, we need a community built," and they sit down and set up some sort of software on their site or they've built a secondary site to act as their forum. They put in too much effort where they're engaged non-stop and it becomes very clear to the initial group that this is going to become almost a dictatorship since anything I do is going to be monitored heavily, edited, and likely to be censored by the company running it.

The flip side is that they don't put enough effort in. If you have ever been the first person at a party, you know that it's a little bit uncomfortable. The only person you have to talk to is the host who is busy trying to make sure that other people greeted as they come in. In other words, you want to make the place comfortable for those initial community members without being too distant or too close.

What's the biggest pitfall the reader may not be aware of?

Todd Herschberg: The biggest pitfall comes a little later once you've gotten that first small group of engaged individuals in your community. Ignoring them can become a tremendous pitfall because these folks are going to be your brand ambassadors. They may view your brand a little differently than you do, but you have to let them have a certain amount of free reign even if it pains you to watch your brand go in a slightly different direction. If you try to bring them back, you risk alienating them causing internal strife and the kinds of things you've seen in just about any forum or community you've been a member of.

How can the reader avoid or overcome this obstacle to successfully achieve and build a thriving community?

Todd Herschberg: The best advice I have for anyone who's gotten to the point where their brand ambassadors are active and engaged in their community, are reaching out to new members, and are acting as your fan club, is to keep them happy. Reward them for doing what they're doing. Give them a special badge in the community--a shout-out on your social media. Make sure they feel really appreciated, and they will continue to be your cheerleaders for a very long time.

What would be the best piece of advice to the reader who's considering building a community?

Todd Herschberg: My personal opinion is to hire Quantimark; but outside of that, you don't necessarily need to bring in a trained group to set everything up. Odds are you already have some members who are active in social media or who are engaged in the brick and mortar world. It could be a celebrity, your next-door neighbor, or any number of people who are really already talking about your brand. Sit down with them, engage with them and say, "Hey, we're going to be setting up a community. What would you like this community to look like?"

If you build a community based on the needs of the people who are already your cheerleaders, they're going to bring in more people like them because you are selling what that customer wants. If you're in the fashion world, for example, you'll find that people will ask you time and time again, "Make sure we have the ability to share images. Make sure we have the ability to talk about your competitors because that is the way we can show why we love your brand over the other." Bringing in these people and letting them help steer your initial direction is invaluable.

What's the first thing the reader should do if they're ready to start building a community, or take an existing community and grow it?

Todd Herschberg: The first thing they should do after they've spoken to their existing cheerleaders is build specifications. There are a million types of communities and there are a million different ways you can run one, whether it's software, real world, a LinkedIn group, a Facebook group, or forum software. Their real needs will direct the route they should take initially. Build out the specs and work with your product people and your project managers. Make sure that the information you've gleaned from your cheerleaders is taken into consideration and becomes a required feature in their future development.

What's the most important thing the reader should think about if they're about to build a community?

Todd Herschberg: The most important thing is how they are going to keep this community engaged and happy. A happy community is a very active and outgoing. They will grow; they will thrive. An unhappy community will devolve into bickering, schisms and flame wars, and all of the things that annoy you if you've spent any time online.

How can the reader find out more about how to build a community?

Todd Herschberg: I'm always happy to spend a couple of minutes on the phone with you. You can pick up the phone and reach me at 213-9-SEARCH. This is the Quantimark main number and I will be happy to spend a few minutes on the phone figuring out what your needs are. I am always happy to give you a little bit of advice or direct you towards someone or some software that may be a better fit for you.

What's the best way for the reader to learn more about your work?

Todd Herschberg: The best way to learn about my work is again to pick up the phone and ask me. I've built many communities over the years and I can show you some examples of communities that have worked and some that haven't. Of course, most of mine have worked, and I can show you how you can best engage your customer. Whether or not you're a client of mine, I'm always happy to spend time because I think that community building is not just good for business, but it's good for keeping people happy and engaged in general. The more happy people there are, the happier the world tends to be.

BIO – Todd Herschberg

Todd Herschberg a seasoned entrepreneur and marketing executive with a heavy emphasis on branding, ecommerce and digital marketing including SEO, SEM, community building and social media. In addition to his frequent speaking engagements and consulting practice, he is one of the most-connected people on LinkedIn, one of FastCompany's 50 Most Influential People Online for 2010 (#33) and the founder of 3 of the 10 largest community groups on Groupsite.com

Todd is an avid community builder - founding OCEAN (Orange County Executives And Networkers), a regional business networking organization with over 12,000 members and co-founding the Fashion Retailers industry group with more than 65,000 members worldwide.

Mr. Herschberg also founded and managed a number of start-up tech firms where he was instrumental in the development and refinement of several search engine technologies and increasing traffic by driving organic traffic via search optimization, community building & digital marketing programs. He was also one of the founders of Albert's Ambry (alberts. com) one of the internet's first specialty software search engines, where he helped to develop both their search algorithms and their fraud control filtering systems

TODD HERSCHBERG

Contact Information:

Phone: 213-9-SEARCH

Email: sales@quantimark.com

Website: www.quantimark.com

Laura J. Lieff

Tell me about Accentuating Service and the types of clients you help.

Laura J. Lieff: Accentuating Service is a coaching and concierge service that specializes in coaching. We provide career, life and dating coaching. The goal of our coaching is to help our clients become more effective in their careers and personal lives so that they are less stressed out. We also serve as part-time or as-needed personal, executive, and virtual assistants. Our goal, in this regard, is to handle the tasks and projects that are on our clients' to-do lists and, by doing so, to help alleviate their stress by providing them with more free time for the people and activities they enjoy.

Describe the clients with whom Accentuating Service works.

Laura J. Lieff: The clients with whom we work are people who need coaching: career, life or dating coaching, or a combination of types of coaching. We work with business leaders who need assistance with leadership skills and who don't have the time to take care of the mundane tasks of daily living. We help others who are, also, very busy and who, therefore, don't have the time to enjoy life. These are people who want to have someone handle the tasks and projects that are on their to-do lists. Our clients aren't, however, required to be very busy or stressed out: we, also, assist people who don't enjoy doing certain tasks and who can afford to have someone else, like us, do those tasks for them.

Please note that, going forward in this chapter, "him" always refers to "her" as well.

What led you to this field?

Laura J. Lieff: One of the things that I enjoyed most about my previous career, legal recruiting, was the coaching aspect of the profession. As I am empathic, practical, realistic, strategic, experienced and optimistic, and as I am a natural advice-giver, coaching is my true calling. My interest in providing concierge services developed over time. Many years ago, while standing on a bank line for a half an hour, it occurred to me that it would be great to have a concierge service do that for me. Several years after that, a friend of mine hired a concierge in southern Florida to pick me up from the airport. The concierge was a charming, friendly person who seemed to enjoy his career choice. As I, most of all, enjoy assisting and inspiring others, and as I like variety, I realized that the most enjoyable work for me would be providing services that combined coaching with concierge work.

How did you get started in coaching?

Laura J. Lieff: I started career coaching, professionally, when I became a legal recruiter, a little over 30 years ago. I have been doing life and dating coaching, as an avocation, for at least 35 years. For more than three decades, I have been involved with helping people become more content in their careers. Since most of us are working longer hours, these days, it is essential that we enjoy what we do for a living. As I have had more than one career and as I have discussed different careers with a wide range of professionals, I am knowledgeable about what various careers are like and, as I keep up with economic and business news, I am aware of which sectors are experiencing rapid growth. Regarding life and dating coaching, by virtue of the facts that I am no longer a young woman and that I have been divorced for many years, I have a lot of life and dating experience and knowledge. As I recently said to a friend, "What's the point of having all this wisdom if I don't share it?" If I can help a client, a relative, a friend, an acquaintance, or even an eavesdropper avoid the anguish and waste of time he is currently experiencing by being focused on a bad situation or an inappropriate person, it gives me a great deal of satisfaction. I hate seeing someone follow an unproductive or frustrating path when I know that, with a little coaching or cheerleading from me, he can become more fulfilled and effective.

How did the concierge service come about?

Laura J. Lieff: One day, it occurred to me that I have many talents, some of which are writing, proofreading and editing, party planning, doing Internet research, coming up with creative solutions to problems, being empathic, providing expert resume and interview prep services, interviewing and hiring contractors, etc. As "Variety is the spice of life", I thought that it would be fun to provide a service that would offer me an opportunity to utilize my various skills while helping others, which is something from which I derive considerable satisfaction.

What's the biggest misconception you might have about coaching?

Laura J. Lieff: The biggest misconception that you might have about coaching is that we are the right professionals to go to for deep-seated psychological problems. The professionals to go to for deep-seated psychological problems are psychologists and, perhaps, psychiatrists as well.

What is the most common obstacle preventing your clients from achieving great outcomes through coaching?

Laura J. Lieff: The most common obstacle preventing my clients from achieving great outcomes through coaching is a lack of open-mindedness or the belief that the only right way to do things is the way they have been doing them for the past ten years or more. Other frequent obstacles are a fear of change and a fear of success. Change is uncomfortable for most people, even though they might know that they need a change or *to* change. Regarding fear of success, although a person might not be happy in his current situation, he is accustomed to it and the idea that he might break out and become successful is, somewhat, threatening to the status quo and to him.

How can you avoid or overcome this obstacle to successfully achieve business leadership through coaching?

Laura J. Lieff: You must be willing to admit to yourself that you don't have all the answers to your career or life issues and that someone else, who has varied and extensive career and life experience, can provide you with another point of view and, also, some very interesting ideas. I have been able to, tactfully, point out to some clients that their career notions, for example, for the past however many years have brought them to the confused and dissatisfied place in which they find themselves today. Therefore, as I tell my clients, it behooves them to let some fresh air into their brains so that they can pull themselves out of the career rut in which they find themselves. The way some of my clients might have avoided their uncomfortable career circumstances is by being more open to getting advice from others with different points of view. With my coaching assistance, some of my clients decided to go back to school to pursue the careers that they are truly interested in pursuing.

What's the biggest pitfall of which you might not be aware?

Laura J. Lieff: Not all coaches are equally effective. The best coach for an individual is the coach with whom that individual feels comfortable, the coach who will be tactful yet truthful, the coach who has a lot of life and/or career experience, and the coach who is kind and empathic. Having a license to coach is nice but it's much less important than truly wanting to help people succeed and having the ability to inspire people to do so. A good coach can create a trusting relationship with his clients by being willing to share his own experiences so that the client understands that most people aren't handed success, but have to work for the success that they achieve.

What would be your best piece of advice to someone who is considering coaching?

Laura J. Lieff: The best advice I can give someone who is considering coaching is to have a consultation with whomever you are interested in hiring, either in person or by telephone, to determine whether you click with that coach. Ask the coach what he brings to the table that is different or better than what other coaches offer. Also, find out how much experience the coach has in the area in which you need coaching. Finally, it can't hurt to read the coach's online reviews, however, you should be aware that there is always someone who will post a negative review mainly because that's the way that person is wired.

What's the first thing you should do if you are ready to start coaching?

Laura J. Lieff: You should make a list of the main issues that you want to discuss in the order of importance to you. After doing that, jot down any questions that you would like to ask the coach. Indicate how you have approached the issues that you are having trouble with, in the past, and how you are dealing with these issues currently. Discuss whether you think that your handling of these issues has improved at all. Ask the coach for more effective ways of dealing with these issues.

What's the most important thing you should think about if you are about to go into coaching?

Laura J. Lieff: If you're about to go into coaching, you need to think about what you hope to gain from it. In other words, what is/are your goal/s for the coaching for which you are paying?

Why might some people who could benefit from coaching decide not to use you for coaching?

Laura Lieff: One thing that might prevent somebody from engaging me for coaching is the fee. Although our coaching services are reasonably priced and well worth the financial investment, not everyone will recognize that. Time commitment might be an issue, as well, and I would say to anyone who is wondering about the time commitment that would be required is that going for coaching is not a lifetime commitment.

The goal of coaching is to help you help yourself. Once you are on the right path, you don't need coaching, anymore, unless you want an occasional check-in session or you need an emergency session. Another obstacle in your mind might be what other people will think. My response regarding that potential obstacle is that people are, generally speaking, too busy dealing with their own problems to have negative thoughts about your going for coaching. In fact, they will probably be interested in knowing how it's going and whether you think that it's helpful. Furthermore, what other people think should be of no consequence to you anyway. I have always felt that what *you* think is more important than what your friends, family or others think. Finally, where is it written that you have to tell others that you are going for coaching?

Another issue might be that you are not convinced that coaching will work for you. Regarding that issue, I would say that you are not signing a long-term contract when you go for coaching. If you try a few sessions and think that it's not for you, you don't have to continue. Another and, perhaps, final obstacle might be that you think that you can do it yourself. My response regarding that perceived obstacle is that if you could do it yourself, you wouldn't be thinking of finding a coach in the first place. Most people find that talking to a professional who is empathic, knowledgeable and objective is helpful. It's not that easy to change destructive or unproductive habits without outside assistance.

How can you find out more about how to use coaching as a leadership tool?

Laura J. Lieff: The best way to find out about how to use coaching as a leadership tool is to jot down the areas in which you're having leadership issues and ask me how I can help you with those areas, i.e., running a business, hiring, interacting with staff, motivating staff, etc.

What's the best way to learn about your work as a coach?

Laura J. Lieff: The best way to learn about my work as a coach is to ask me and/or to request the contact information of prior coaching clients of mine.

If the reader thinks they might be ready to, how can they connect with you?

Laura J. Lieff: Please call me at (212) 688-6506 if you can use advice or coaching regarding how to be an effective leader or about anything else. If you are having career, life or dating issues with which you can use assistance or if you are in a rut in one or more areas of your life, call or email me and I will respond at my earliest opportunity. A half-hour complimentary consultation, by telephone, is available to you so that you can decide whether we're a good fit.

BIO – Laura J. Lieff

Laura J. Lieff, the president of Accentuating Service, launched her concierge and coaching company in April, 2013. Prior to that time, she was president of M/L Legal Search Inc., the legal recruiting company that she founded in November, 1996. At her legal recruiting company, Laura placed attorneys into law firms worldwide. She was a legal recruiter for almost 30 years. Laura has prior experience as an advertising executive of a top New York advertising agency and as administrative assistant to a Senior Vice President of a major publishing company. She has other business experience as well.

Laura has a B.A. in English from Brooklyn College. She was a licensed high school English teacher, upon graduation, at the age of 20.

Laura's clients would describe her as being client-oriented, responsible and reliable, very intelligent, empathic, professional, and honest. None of them has regretted using her coaching services and they indicated that they had been exposed to, at least, one useful idea or piece of information which helped them to handle their issue/s more effectively.

Laura's interests include the following: spending time with family and friends, socializing, business, golf and tennis, movies, music, the other arts, travel, nature and humor. Most of all, she enjoys assisting, encouraging and inspiring others. Laura is a creative and strategic thinker who truly loves what she does for a living.

Contact Information:

Web site: www.AccentuatingService.com

Email: AccentuatingService@gmail.com

Cell phone: 212.688.6506

Jane Tabachnick

Tell me about Jane Tabachnick & Co. and the types of customers you help?

Jane Tabachnick: Jane Tabachnick & Co. is a digital media and publishing agency that creates Authority Positioning – helping entrepreneurs and professionals become the go to experts in their niche. I help them get more visibility, establish instant credibility and recognition, and attract a steady stream of pre-sold clients. I also have an independent publishing house called Simply Good Press, which helps experts become published, bestselling authors. My team and I provide mentoring, training, and workshops for individuals and companies that want to conduct their own marketing and promotion. I provide the tools to empower them to make better, informed decisions, even when running their own campaigns and when hiring outsourcers to handle their implementation.

Describe the clients Jane Tabachnick and Co. works with?

Jane Tabachnick: The type of customers we help ranges from start-ups to existing businesses ready to take their business to the next level. Our clients are solopreneurs, coaches, small businesses, and professionals. The coaches include executive coaches, and health and wellness coaches, as well as other types. I work with lawyers, doctors, and accountants, as well as professional service firms or providers.

Many of our clients are heart-centered entrepreneurs. I will work with anyone seeking more visibility as the go to expert in his or her niche. I like to say that we help our clients become the hunted, rather than the hunter; thus we turn them into client attraction magnets. This works for anyone who has just started a business and who wants to establish instant credibility and more visibility. Authority marketing and expert author programs are ideal to accomplish this. For the businesses that are ready to take off, our program provides rocket fuel-giant boost and leverage-that helps them get to the next level quickly.

Jane Tabachnick & Co, and Simply Good Press work with any company with a marketing budget that invests in marketing and promotion and is serious about positioning themselves as the top in their niche.

What led you to this field?

Jane Tabachnick: I started out as a fashion designer in my own business. Like most entrepreneurs, I wore a number of hats in addition to the design and manufacturing of proprietary designs. I handled all the marketing and publicity for my firm. I found that I was not only good at it, but that I really enjoyed it. When I decided to get out of the business, I took stock of my skills and my passion and realized that I loved and preferred doing the creative marketing, publicity, and buzz building.

When I discovered the Internet, I knew it was going to be a phenomenal tool for marketing and promotion and it hasn't proved me wrong yet. Early on, I was building websites for clients, I continually saw that one of the biggest challenges that our clients had was not being found by their target audience. To me, this reinforced the importance of getting visibility in front of ideal prospects. Shortly thereafter, I had the opportunity of participating in a big online promotional event where I was invited to create an info product as part of giveaways and products for sale. I took my passion for creating buzz and created my first book, Plain Jane Promotional Planner. It sold well and generated some nice publicity on its own without much effort on my part. I haven't looked back since.

How did you get started in this business?

Jane Tabachnick: After leaving the fashion business and working for a small advertising agency in New Jersey, I was enjoying great success. I was intrigued with the state-of-the-art large format and digital printing equipment in house, as well as the digital photography studio. When I discovered the Internet, I was so excited about it that I went to the president of the company and suggested that we create websites for clients. It was a perfect complement to the graphic design and branding work we already were doing. We had all the logos and graphics we had developed which we were storing on their behalf.

Our clients trusted us and loved working with us. Doing website design (which was going to be an important marketing piece for every business in the not-so-distant future) would be a natural addition to the services the agency was offering. I suggested to the president that we hire or partner with a software developer to work on the backend, doing the technical aspect of the website. It made sense because our clients would expect us to design the look and feel of their site to match their brands. The president wasn't interested in going in this direction at that time however.

I felt that the Web was something I had to become involved in. I felt so strongly about it that I left the company and took a job with a Web development and interactive multimedia agency. I sat next to the developers and probably drove them crazy asking a lot of questions: why are you doing this? How does that work? I was, and still am, eternally curious. I like to peek under the hood and understand how things work. Even if I'm not going to be doing the coding or the backend work, I feel that it informs my decisions and helps me advise my clients better. That job was not meant to be long term, so I went out on my own, creating my first digital agency called Strategy.

How did you get started in marketing and PR?

Jane Tabachnick: During the time I was a fashion designer, I needed to get the word out about my designs and began doing promotion. In addition, there were times when I was looking to work for one of the biggest design firms. I felt the best way to get in the door was to use some kind of unique marketing campaign for myself rather than just send out my resume or portfolio.

When you are in a creative field, people expect to see you demonstrate your creativity in a way comes across as well as the way you dress and present yourself. I used some very creative strategies and got a number of meetings with the big name companies I was trying to land a position with. I had fun coming up with these marketing strategies, which we're also getting results. I believe it was at this time that I was first called the Idea Factory.

From the beginning of my career, I had begun volunteering with an organization called the American Woman's Economic Development Corps, or AWED. I started out volunteering to help run workshops for women entrepreneurs, and over time I was hired as a consultant to create conferences to help teach them how to use technology in their businesses.

The staff would ask me how to get the word out about the events. This is a skill I used a number of times both with AWED and other organizations I worked with to help promote events or initiatives. I am self-taught, as I have never taken any formal classes in marketing. I should say haven't taken formal classes at a university. I have undergone many training programs and have worked with marketing and PR coaches to develop and fine-tune my skills.

How did the current Authority Marketing service come about?

Jane Tabachnick: My business has evolved over time. I focused on publicity, digital marketing, publicity mentoring and developing promotion and marketing-related services and tools. I never really wanted to run a full service PR firm; however, clients were always looking for a solution. One of the biggest challenges in selling PR services is that it takes a while to build up momentum, build relationships with the media and start getting results. This can be frustrating to clients.

It can also be a very tough sell to say to a client "you need to pay me a lot of money, a minimum of a six month retainer, and I can't guarantee you any results" or "I can't tell you what the results will be, however we will get some results." I had been looking for a solution to provide some of the same benefits, but where I knew I could guarantee results and deliver them fairly quickly. I tried a few things but just had not found the right service. Then I discovered authority marketing. In a nutshell, it is at the intersection of content marketing and publicity. By strategically placing content on high profile websites and then promoting that content often via a press release, it has the same effect for a client as publicity. The interesting side to it is that it often seeds what I think of as traditional publicity.

So Authority Marketing helps attract the media who are happy to see that you've already gotten some "coverage: and know how to work with them, an important factor. It's been a great service; people love the results and I enjoyed delivering them.

What's the biggest misconception the reader may have about authority marketing and public relations?

Jane Tabachnick: Many people don't understand publicity, content marketing, or authority marketing completely. They often expect press or content marketing to look like an advertisement. However, it's subtler than that. The media wants to tell stories that interest their audience, and you need to find a way to make your company or product fit into their story or style... not the other way around.

The misconception is that anyone cares about what you say about your business. We are in a review economy – people look to friends and family; they seek out online reviews, and they trust the media to provide third-party credibility and confirmation that you are quality, reputable and real. Prospects would come to me with very specific and very unattainable expectations – or at least not in the instant timeframe they wanted. I would not guarantee that I could get them into a specific publication within a stated time frame.

I have explained to prospects that if you want to be in a specific publication on a specific page and placement on a particular date, then you need to take out an ad. This is just one example of some of the misconceptions about how the media and publicity work. I think that one of the most important things you can do in running your company and providing successful outcomes for your clients is to manage expectations. Unfortunately, I have had to turn away clients or prospects because I didn't feel that their expectations were realistic, and I would much rather under-promise and over-deliver than to disappoint.

What is the most common obstacle preventing the reader from achieving great outcomes through authority marketing and publicity?

Jane Tabachnick: I've said this before and I'll quote it again, like the New York State Lottery ad campaign; you have to be in it to win it. You have to be actively or proactively doing marketing and promotion if you wanted reap the benefits. This may sounds simplistic, but there are entrepreneurs who don't even try to do any promotion or get more visibility for themselves. I've also come across clients who are either introverted or publicity shy. It can be more challenging for them to seek out publicity if they're not comfortable in the spotlight.

This became evident to me in some of the one-on-one sessions or group coaching I was conducting with clients. It took me a while to understand exactly what was going on and why. I had clients who came to me knowing they wanted and needed to do publicity and promote their business; yet I felt they were resisting and that something was stopping them from doing everything I was teaching them to do to get the visibility they deserved.

BUSINESS LEADERSHIP BLUEPRINTS

I have seen that one can realize the value of publicity and getting more visibility and still either fear it or have some things that hold them back from doing it.

This led me to write the book, Publicity for Introverts. It also led me to develop a coaching program specifically designed for introverts, or the spotlight shy, to help them do publicity in a way that can become comfortable for them so they won't resist doing it, so they can get in front of more ideal clients. Thinking like this can be an obstacle to doing your own publicity or even having a firm do it on your behalf. Some people have a mindset that either it's scary and overwhelming or that there is only a one-size-fits-all approach. It can be a limiting mindset that holds people back from doing publicity and getting the kind of results that would catapult their business in the way they desire. It can also be lack of skills and training--not knowing the rules of the road or having a roadmap, not knowing how to start or what to do next.

What's the biggest pitfall the reader may not be aware of?

Jane Tabachnick: The biggest pitfall is what may be holding people back from doing PR: that's number one. I think PR, in particular, can be very intimidating as people think you need a high-price firm or it's too complicated to learn or too scary to approach a journalist--or all the above. However, it's really fairly simple to learn what PR is and how it works. The fact of the matter is that journalists are people, and if you know how to work with them and you come up with good story ideas and you pick the right ones, then they will be very welcoming and receptive, and you will probably get publicity. Maybe not on the first foray, but it probably won't take long.

The other obstacle that people have is not understanding the difference between publicity, marketing, and advertising. Publications and their audiences want to tell great stories about people and companies. They want to feature stories that their audience can care about. One of the biggest pitfalls people have is not stepping into the shoes or mindset of the end user--the reader of the publication as well as the journalist. They should ask why they would care about me and then craft a story along the lines instead of thinking, how can I talk about my business and get myself free press.

How can the reader avoid or overcome this obstacle to successfully achieve business leadership through public relations?

Jane Tabachnick: I think most people understand the value of being visible to their target audience. That said, it's important to have other people sing your praises, such as the media. One of the best ways to be seen as a leader, besides acting like a leader and publishing thought leadership, is to have other people speak about you positively. This offers third-party credibility. Being featured in the media instantly positions you as a top expert in your niche or field.

To avoid or overcome the obstacles mentioned, it's important to understand first of all how PR works. Then it's important to understand what I call your PR Persona™. Whether you are an extrovert, an ambivert, an introvert, or just publicity shy, there are ways you can do publicity that won't make you uncomfortable. For example, if you don't like being on camera, no matter how much training or encouragement you get, you are not going to want to be on camera. That's not part of your PR persona.

However, for those who either love being on camera or are willing to get some coaching and practice because they feel the value is worth any initial discomfort, then more power to them. They can add being on camera to their PR persona™ and strategy. Once you have these two things in place, understanding how the media works and knowing your PR persona™, then you can hire a PR firm on retainer.

It is important to get some training and or coaching in PR whatever your decision so you can be more successful with it. Additionally, training, knowledge, and even practice, build confidence. If you are looking to do more public speaking, or if you are looking to do more interviews, you might want to start speaking in front of small groups rather than keynoting a 500 or 2000 person conference. The success you feel and what you achieve by speaking to small groups helps to build your muscles and your knowledge. It will give you the confidence to do it on a larger scale.

What would be your best piece of advice to the reader who is considering publicity or authority marketing?

Jane Tabachnick: The best advice I can give is to learn what PR is and how it works. Information and knowledge is power. You also want to get at a minimum some basic training in the subject. This will give you the knowledge you need, as well as additional confidence, so you won't come across as uninformed or embarrassed. No one wants to feel that way, like the newbie or new recruit. You can easily do your own PR or have someone on your team do it and outsource those tasks that either are not your skill set or require an advanced one.

The other advice I would give is to start building relationships with journalists. First you need to know what your audience reads: what publications, blogs, and websites. This is the first step to understanding what publications to target that can help put you in front of your ideal audience. And believe it or not, I speak to a lot of clients who don't know what their audience reads.

This is a very basic and informative piece of information you want to have about your target audience. Once you know what they read, and where they spend their time, you can then start to develop relationships with the right journalists. I am not telling you to pitch them about you and your company. What I'm recommending is to connect with them on social media; share their stories, like their stories, retweet their stories. This will help put you on their radar so that when you are ready to pitch them, your name will be familiar and they'll be receptive.

What's the first thing the reader should do if they are ready to start a PR program?

Jane Tabachnick: If you're ready to start a marketing or promotional program, it's important to evaluate your goals and timeline. It helps to know your budget as well. You must understand at least partly how you would like to accomplish your objectives. Do you want to take a totally hands-off approach and outsource the entire program? Perhaps you want someone to help come up with a strategy and then guide you through some of the implementation. Or perhaps you would prefer to have someone like me mentor you so that you have the skills and tools you need to do the promotional campaign on your own in-house. Once you have identified all these factors, you can begin to seek out the right professional consultant or service firm to help you achieve your goals.

What's the most important thing the reader should think about if they are about to go into a PR or authority marketing program?

Jane Tabachnick: It's important to understand the buyer persona. If you're not familiar with this concept, it refers to the different personalities, interests and focus of your prospect at each point along the sales cycle, from the moment that they first hear about your company through various touch points, until they actually buy and become a customer. Understanding this can help you determine the kind of marketing, messaging and promotion you will want to do. Doing this first will help you achieve greater success with your campaign because you will have begun with a lot more information and you'll be able to custom-tailor the campaign to specific points along the buyer's journey. You will see how quickly they move forward towards becoming a customer.

If you are not familiar with this process, you can work with an outside consultant such as myself to help guide you through it. I'm a certified HubSpot inbound marketing consultant with expertise in buyer personas. A consultant can help lend a fresh perspective and an objective voice to the process, especially if it's one with which you're not familiar.

The other area that is important to be aware of before you start your promotional campaign is where your customers spend their time online, meaning which social media networks they prefer and visit frequently, as well as which publications they read. This may sound simple and obvious; however, as mentioned earlier, I speak with many individuals and even companies who don't know the answer to this question.

To maximize the return on investment of any program, you want to make sure that you are promoting and gaining visibility on the right media channels and outlets in order to give you the best possible exposure in front of your target audience. There are so many channels to choose from and you can't be everywhere and do it well, unless perhaps you have the kind of budget that a Disney or Kraft Foods has. So it pays to be selective and focus on those channels that are most popular with your audience.

How can the reader find out more about how to use authority marketing and publicity as a leadership tool?

Jane Tabachnick: To find out more about using authority marketing and publicity as a leadership too, there is a lot of great information online, including great publications like the Harvard Business Review, Entrepreneur, Inc., Forbes, and a number of more niche blogs that all have great content. I write about authority marketing, content marketing, getting visibility and publicity, and becoming an author on my blog; I am also a guest expert on other blogs. My website also has some recording of podcast interviews I have given on these topics. Podcasts are also a great way to learn from experienced thought leaders and companies. You have to find people who resonate with you, who are having their own success, and then you follow them.

What's the best way for the reader to learn more about your work?

Jane Tabachnick: Thank you for asking! There is a good amount of information on my website at JaneTabachnick.com. I have a blog where I write about publicity, content marketing and the customer experience. I offer some complimentary reports you can download. The website also offers information about my services, past projects, clients I've worked with, and just about any other information you may be looking for. If you feel you're ready to get started, then you can reach out to me and set up a time to speak with me. There are also some interviews I have done on the radio and various podcasts you can listen to that are listed on my website.

If the reader thinks they might be ready to, how can they connect with you?

Jane Tabachnick: First visit my website and start with the section called Work With Me. You can have a look at some of the packages I offer to give you a sense of the scope of my work. If you know you are ready to get started, you can reach out to me via my website at http://www.janetabachnick.com/contact or give me a call at 646-867-0788. I will be more than happy to speak with you about the possibility of working together. I offer complimentary strategy sessions. It's important for us to explore whether it's a good fit to work together. It also gives me a chance to learn more about your business and goals. With that knowledge, I can make the best recommendation as to how to get the most visibility and get in front of ideal clients.

BIO – Jane Tabachnick

Jane Tabachnick is digital public relations and marketing strategist and mentor. She brings 20 years of experience working with savvy entrepreneurs and business owners to position them as the top expert in their niche, create greater visibility and buzz, which helps them easily attract and close more of their ideal customers.

Passionate about entrepreneurship, Jane has been instrumental in creating programs, courses and tools to empower entrepreneurs with up to date knowledge and resources so that they can succeed. She is the creator of the Sustainable Design Entrepreneur's Program at New York's Fashion Institute of Technology, where she is also an adjunct professor.

Jane was honored with a Galaxy Award for her work with women entrepreneurs, and has been named one of the Top 100 People Online by FastCompany. Jane and her clients have been featured or quoted in, Clickz, Crains, ABC, CBS, The NY Enterprise Report, The Star Ledger, Environmental Leader, CNN, Houston Magazine, Spa Magazine, Women's Wear Daily and many other media outlets.

Authority Bar plug-in, Instant Pressroom plug-in, and Easy Author One Sheets are a few of the do it yourself marketing and publicity tools that Jane has created.

Jane is the founder of Simply Good Press, a publishing house that helps experts become published, bestselling authors. She is the author of Publicity for Introverts. She has completed the Dublin [Ireland] Marathon, and is working on perfecting gluten free baking in her spare time.

You can also download her free report from her website: **10 Ways Becoming an Author Will Make You Money**

Contact Information:

Web site: www.janetabachnick.com

www.simplygoodpress.com

Email: jane@janetabachnick.com

Phone: 646 867- 0788

Conclusion

5 unique leaders and 5 leadership blueprints, which share common traits as well as unique aspects and approaches. A customer-focused orientation seems to be the heart of the matter for the five leaders interviewed in this book. They all have services to offer that require a deep client focus and an understanding of specific and unique client needs. A drive to serve and help their audience solve some of their greatest challenges has propelled each of these leaders to personal success. In every case, their success means their clients achieve success. Another ingredient in all cases is drive and ambition. They set out with a goal and succeeded by dint of will power, talent, and dedication to their cause.

In every case, surrounding yourself with the right people is a key ingredient for success, whether it's a mentor, a teacher or your very own clients. As Blane clearly states it,

"The kind of people I like to work with are creatives. To me, a creative leader is anyone who creates anything. It's not only an artist and it doesn't have to be an actor or a director or a painter. Anyone who has an idea and has the guts to go out on a limb and try something and really commit to it, are the kind of people I like to work with."

Helping others is a big factor in the leadership equation. With Jeffrey M. Bloom, the target audience is leaders who seek to improve their productivity and influence. "I have the ability to meet with decision makers and talk about their goals. I ask, what is your organization's culture and what would you like it to be? What do you see happening next year, in five years, or ten years and beyond? Then I tailor a program of seminar(s) or an on-going training. I have the experience and ability to follow up with an accountability program to ensure that the goals and outcomes that were important, along with the new policies and procedures put into place, are being used effectively."

The point is to find a niche in each case that speaks to human needs, while drawing out the best of oneself in the process. As Laura Lieff confesses, "If I can help a client, relative, friend, acquaintance, or even an eavesdropper avoid the anguish and waste of time he is currently experiencing by being focused on a bad situation or an inappropriate person, it gives me a great deal of satisfaction. I hate seeing someone follow an unproductive or frustrating path when I know that, with a little coaching or cheerleading from me, he can become more fulfilled and effective."

Building community and consensus are also traits of great leaders. Jeffrey M. Bloom does this skillfully via his mediation skills, whether helping a couple resolve differences, or helping employees and companies resolve conflict and find solutions that work for both parties

Todd Herschberg builds communities online to benefit interest groups, companies and brands. Todd uses his masterful understanding of technology and social media and SEO, as well as human nature to rapidly build communities of active, engaged users. He does this via his laser like insight into what drives a community, inspires people to get involved and to contribute to the growth of the community, cajoling even the shyest of members to contribute and participate. This empowers both the community and its individual members to have not just a feeling of belonging but also a sense of ownership and pride amongst the collective group, creating a strong and thriving community with long-term stickiness.

Offering guidance can be on a one-to-one or large scale, or anything in between. In every case, the benefits are legion to all concerned: the reward is in the service to others by leading the way. There is always an eye on achievement that is selfless and outer directed. It can be a business executive or an entire corporation: the process is the same.

In Jeffrey's words, "Successful corporations know the value of leadership; in particular, transformational leadership in which they are putting into place effective training programs that result in significant and positive change. Higher and more effective leadership happens through change and by learning, understanding and implementing effective concepts to not only influence people, but to really understand what the corporate culture. The number one thing here is creating value for your people."

Creating value is indeed a common buzzword among successful entrepreneurs. It has to do with identifying just the right strategies that complement specific needs and objectives. It means giving the best of yourself to a set of goals that beckon workable solutions. These five individuals are practical and yet visionary. They know how to go beyond fundamentals to reach deeper results. You might say that they are gifted in their ability to discern what works and what does not, and are willing to try, to fail and fail again until they come up with the best possible solution.

Reading between the lines yields evidence of a directing mind that enriches others. According to Jane Tabachnick, "Some people have a mindset that either it's [public relations] scary and overwhelming or that there is only a one-size-fits-all approach. It can be a limiting mindset that holds people back from doing [publicity] and getting the kind of results that would catapult their business in the way they desire. It can also be lack of skills and training--not knowing the rules of the road or having a roadmap, not knowing how to start or what to do next." It is up to Jane to lead the way.

Also in common is the ability to ask the right questions in order to delve into a rich unknown where purpose and conviction reside. Asking questions around fundamental issues allows these leaders to know their clients better and to develop a methodology that works whether it is a couple in mediation for Jeffrey, a corporate leader needing visual branding and help telling his story for Blane, community building for Todd, the introverted publicity shy client for Jane, or individuals who need coaching for Laura. In all cases, knowing how to listen, and what to listen for, is half the battle in obtaining results. It is all about empathy, understanding, and complete transference of interest.

The final ingredient that permeates this group is passion or a deep commitment to what they do. They demonstrate that no matter what your ambition, it will not reach its mark without a strong dose of desire and engagement. In effect, they attach themselves to a cause and take it forward at its own pace. Each of these talented entrepreneurs has the ability to customize their work and address the needs of individuals, not abstractions. The book, in effect, is a primer on resolving problems and wielding influence so that others can shine. It is the best kind of stimulation and motivation. As Jeffrey wisely states it, "results can only change, when action changes." Leadership is guiding people and teams toward that action.

www.ingramcontent.com/pod-product-compliance
Lightning Source LLC
Chambersburg PA
CBHW060621200326
41521CB00007B/841